Coaching
For The
BUSY! Woman

La Rhonda Crosby-Johnson

Get It Girl Publishing
San Francisco, California

Coaching for the Busy Woman/La Rhonda Crosby-Johnson—First Edition
Ordering Information:
For information about bulk purchases, please contact La Rhonda Crosby-Johnson at larhondawrites@gmail.com.

Tradeback ISBN: 979-8-9851228-2-4

Printed in the United States of America
US Copyright Office: https://copyright.gov/

Dedicated to Phyllida Burlingame

One BUSY! Woman

Coaching For The BUSY! Woman was birthed in 2013 from a conversation with a colleague and friend. She was a single mom of two school-aged children, navigating leadership in her organization and facilitating important community work. She was feeling over extended and overwhelmed. During lunch together, she stated that she was struggling to find time for herself. I had recently decided to take my transformational (life) coaching business to a new level and heard her words in a way I may not have otherwise. On my ride home, I realized that the intentional time needed to commit to a traditional coaching program was not available to my friend. In that moment, I realized that she was probably not alone. I asked myself, "What can I do to support these women?" And Coaching For The BUSY! Woman was born.

In the initial offering, it was distributed as a weekly email subscription. Several years later, for a brief time, it was offered as a downloadable journal.

Coaching For The BUSY! Woman now has a new life. I hope it allows you to create enough room for yourself in your own life. Divided into weekly installments of reflection and encouragement, CFTBW makes room for YOU!

La Rhonda Crosby-Johnson
January 9, 2025

Also by La Rhonda Crosby-Johnson

Fiction

The Jubilee Taylor Series
A Name That Sang
Buttermilk and Baseball
At Last: Jubilee's Song

Unveiled

Natural Nia

Non-Fiction/Essays

"Until Jesus Comes Back"
From the anthology *Life's Spices From Seasoned Sistahs*

"Polka-Dots and Lipstick"
From the anthology *More of Life's Spices: Seasoned Sistahs Keepin' It Real*

"Dear Michelle"
From the anthology *Go, Tell Michelle: African American Women Write to the New First Lady*

"Why We 40-ish Sistahs Welcome The Fifties With Open Arms"
From the anthology *Savvy, Sassy and Bold After 50! A Midlife Rebirth*

"From Negro to Black"
From the anthology *All The Women In My Family Sing*

"Perhaps all the dragons in our lives are princesses who are only waiting to see us act, just once, with beauty and courage. Perhaps everything that frightens us, in its deepest essence, is something helpless that wants our love."
-Rainer Maria Rilke

"If we know ourselves, we're always home anywhere."
-Glinda The Good Witch of The South (from The Wiz)

"There are years that ask questions and years that answer."
-Zora Neale Hurston

Week 1
"The stick that is to save you is found in your hand."
-African Proverb

It is NEVER "them", "him" or "her." What you think is the problem is not. It is merely a symptom; that part of the iceberg that peaks above the water. The real work we must do to be well is ALWAYS below the surface.

Life Tool: For the next 7 days, at least once a day, state and/or acknowledge without excuse, explanation or wavering how you feel. Ask for what you need clearly and without apology. Use I – Messages and avoid attack methods of communicating by avoiding blaming and criticizing.

Remember IT IS YOU THAT "IT" IS ABOUT.

~MEDITATION~

Reading
"Phenomenal Woman" and "Still I
Rise" by Maya Angelou (poems)

Music
"I Choose", "Just Do You" and "Strength, Wisdom and
Courage" by India. Arie

Movie
"The Wizard of Oz." and "The
Wiz"

Week 1

Week 2
"Just your existence proves the existence of God."
-Don Miguel Ruiz

I first became familiar with the term "self-esteem" in the mid-1980's. It almost seems that the recognition of the term made us feel badly about ourselves. "Do I have enough self-esteem?" "Is my self-esteem-high enough?" It is easy (and SO VERY HUMAN) to see scarcity and lack. It is easy to hold your head down and stumble through life worrying about being "good enough." Well, today you can live differently. Hold your head up and walk like you are the finest work of The Creator.

Life Tool: For the next 7 days reduce your criticism of others. Avoid talking about what people look like, what they're wearing, what they are doing 'wrong' in their lives, what you and others "should" or "should not" do. Focus on finding the best in others and yourself.

~MEDITATION~

Reading
"Healing Rage"
by Ruth King, M.A.

Music
"Superwoman"
by Alicia Keys

Movie
"Grand Canyon"

Week 2

Week 3
"The greatest thing a woman can find for herself is her own way." -La Rhonda Crosby-Johnson

Cinderella, Jasmine and Tiana are Disney Characters! STOP waiting for someone (your prince, fully equipped with white horse or BMW) or something (a new outfit, job, car, weave, house, etc.) to save you. You have everything you need to save yourself. Be courageous enough to find your own way. Open yourself up to unlimited possibilities. Look your faults and fears in the face and walk right past them. Forgive yourself for EVERYTHING you did or did not do that displeases you. Tell yourself the truth about your brilliance and as Marianne Williamson says, "Stop playing small." Whether barefoot or wearing shoes with bright red bottoms, stand up, Girl!

Life Tool: For the next 7 days, once per day, write something you'd like to do or experience (don't worry about if you have the time, money, etc.) Now develop a plan of action to accomplish it!

~MEDITATION~

Reading
"Circle of Stones"
by Judith Duerk

Music
"Dusk"
by Jim Chappell

Movie
""Angels In The Outfield"

Week 3

Week 4
"There are accidental parents. There are no accidental babies. -Rick Warren

STOP blaming your children for the life you're not living. Stop asking them to fill the empty spaces inside you. Stop disguising your anger, disappointment, and regret as "sacrifice" and expecting it to control the behaviors of your children as they grow. Sometimes our children arrive before we are prepared for them. Whose fault would that be? Right. Ours. Instead of punishing yourself (by blaming, denying and avoiding) and them (by withholding love, forcing them to fulfill your needs, etc.) learn what they came here to teach you about yourself .One of my favorite African Proverbs says, "Children are the reward of life." Today, begin to see them this way. Treat them this way. It doesn't matter if they are 3 days, 3 months or 3 decades old. You may just discover how great a parent you are....now if you're reading this and are not a parent; know that no matter when you showed up in your parent's life, YOU WERE ON TIME. You came to do what you were designed to do – whether or no they were joyously awaiting your arrival or stressing about how they would care for you. So, stop behaving like you are here by chance. Show up for your life.

Life Tool: Parents - For the next 7 days, once per day, have a conversation about parenting with your parents, children, and friends. Talk about the joys and challenges. Nor Parents - Write a letter or make a call to your parent(s) sharing what it was like being parented by them.

~MEDITATION~

Reading
"Until Today" and "Acts of Faith"
by Iyanla Vanzant

Music
"I'm Coming Out"
by Diana Ross

Movie
"Pleasantville"

Week 4

Week 5
"I'll never be perfect, but at least now I'm brave."
-Alicia Keys

Perfection is not the goal. Stop killing yourself to reach it. Stop judging others for not fitting your idea of perfection. Make bravery your goal. Face each day and circumstance with the courage it takes to "get through it", "rise above it." Being brave doesn't mean you won't be afraid. Being brave is admitting when you are afraid and trusting that you'll come out okay.

Life Tool: For the next 7 days when you feel yourself backing away, delaying or avoiding a conversation or situation, take a deep breath. Ask yourself the question, "What scares me about this?" and then move through it, trusting that you are already courageous enough for the task.

~MEDITATION~

Reading
Hebrews 11:1 and Psalm 23
(The Bible)

Music
"Salt"
by Lizz Wright

Movie
"The Karate Kid"
(Either the original or Jaden Smith version)

Week 5

Week 6
"Just because we cannot see the whole path doesn't mean it's not there." –Fana (a character from the novel, My Soul To Take.)

FAITH. Ever wonder if you've got enough? Having faith doesn't mean you won't wonder about the outcome, hesitate before you take the first step, question or even doubt yourself. Don't let your questions about your level of faith make you give up on yourself. Don't define who you are by what may be going on in or around you. Don't allow yourself to believe that because tears cloud your vision or pain grips your heart that there are not better days ahead. Just keep putting one foot in front of the other. Faith is trusting and believing that even when you cannot see your way, your way exists.

Life Tool: For the next 7 days reduce your need to know every outcome. Get in the car and just drive. Pick up a book by an unfamiliar writer. Make that decision you've been losing sleep over.

~MEDITATION~

Reading
"The Gifts of Imperfection" and "Daring Greatly"
by Brene Brown

Music
"Individuality"
by Rachelle Ferrell

Movie
"Tuesdays With Morrie""

Week 6

Week 7

"All stress comes from resisting what is."
-Oprah Winfrey

What's hiding in the bottom drawer? What do you have pushed to the back of the closet? What are you denying each time you look in the mirror? What are you telling yourself and others about what you're hiding? Why you're hiding? The energy you are using to hide will be better spent bringing everything out in the open. I know. You've had it hidden for years. I know. If you tell "them" the truth they might not like/love/invite you to Christmas dinner. I know. And it's scary and you could get hurt. But aren't you already hurting?

Life Tool: For the next 7 days, tell the truth about what you're feeling, what your experience is in any given situation. Resist the habit of saying what you think others want you to say; feeling what you think others expect you to feel.

~MEDITATION~

Reading
"The Color Purple"
by Alice Walker

Music
"Best Self"
by Lady Bri

Movie
"The Women of Brewster Place"

Week 7

Week 8

"Love doesn't use a fist. Love never calls you fat or lazy or ugly. Love doesn't laugh at you in front of your friends... Love does not maintain a list of your flaws and weaknesses. Love believes you." -Augusten Burroughs

It's time we get a better grip on this "love thang." What does your love look like? How does it make you and those around you feel? Are you using all your love trying to get somebody else to love you? Are you spending enough time loving yourself? Are we using "love" as a weapon to cause someone else pain or as a treat to be doled out until we get what we want? Love has no strings attached. It doesn't require that we wait to be loved first. We've all suffered some pain because what love meant to us didn't mean the same thing to the one(s) we loved. Love doesn't hurt. I found it interesting that when studying Yoruba language and culture, they didn't have a word for love. They consider the word "love" to be a verb. It is seen in our interactions with others. So again, what does your love look like?

Life Tool – This week spend some time each day creating a working definition of love.Make it concrete, so you recognize it when it shows up. Try this:Ask yourself, "If I am loving (or being loved) what does it look like, sound like, feel like (or make the other person feel.) This week don't just talk love, BE LOVING!

~MEDITATION~

Reading
"Feel The Fear and Do It Anyway"
by Susan Jeffers, Ph.D.

Music
"Even Angels"
by Fantasia

Movie
"Steel Magnolias"
(Either the Sally Field or Queen Latifah version will work.)

Week 8

Week 9
"The ruin of a nation begins in the homes of its people."
-African Proverb

Time to take a look at your house. Not just your physical house, but your spiritual and emotional house. Are things not going the way you want them at work?Are your relationships in a state of disrepair? Look in the house. We will fail at solving the problems of the world, if we can't figure out how to connect to ourselves and those around us. It is easier to sit back and wait for someone else to "fix it", "solve it", and "make it better." Well, guess what? You're it.Haven't hugged your own children or had a conversation with them that didn't involve an electronic device?Well, then stop talking about the kids hanging out on the corner or acting up in the classroom. There is no shame in admitting brokenness. Don't stop there, just talking about what isn't working. Move toward solutions. Look inside when outside isn't going your way.

Life Tool: For the next 7 days connect. Call someone who's been "on your mind." Turn off the television and sit quietly with yourself.Fix a meal with the folks that live in the house with you and then sit down and eat it together. Ask a co-worker how they're doing and wait for an answer.

~MEDITATION~

Reading
"Women, Food and God: An Unexpected Path to Almost Everything"
by Geneen Roth

Music
"Shine"
by Laura Izibor

Movie
"The Trip To Bountiful"
(Starring Geraldine Page or Cicely Tyson)

Week 9

Week 10
"There is not an obstacle available that doesn't have an opportunity preceding it." –Beverly Kearney.

It is only after the "storm" has passed that we begin to celebrate. We spend time and energy trying to avoid storms or sitting and moaning during the storm. The next time a storm appears, open your eyes, mind and heart. It is filled with information for us; things we've missed or overlooked, new ways of being and doing things, lessons that improve our lives and the lives of those around us.If the obstacle has presented itself there are a few things that could be going on: 1) time for you to build some new skills and get out of your comfort zone, 2) time to use the tools/skills you learned from the last storm, 3) time to reflect and evaluate, 4) time to express gratitude.

Life Tool: For the next seven days, review your "storm" list.What did you learn? What did you stop doing or start doing to get through the storm?What differences did you notice once the storm had passed? Was it useful in predicting future storms?

~MEDITATION~

Reading
"From The Heart: Seven Rules To Live By"
by Robin Roberts

Music
"The Answer To Why"
by Ledisi

Movie
"The Single Mom's Club"

Week 10

Week 11
"Choice is a divine teacher, for when we choose, we learn that nothing is ever put in our path without reason." –Iyanla Vanzant

There is power in choosing. We get hundreds of opportunities to choose every day. You've probably already made at least 20 choices already today. There is always a choice. Yes, I said always. Sometimes there's not a lot to choose from. Sometimes the choice will mean leaving something or someone behind. Sometimes the choice is just plain old hard. But there is always a choice and choosing for yourself is always better than allowing someone else to choose for you. Remember not making a choice is a choice not to use your power; direct your own life.

Life Tool: This week make choices; review the choices you've made in the past. Allow others to make their own choices, too.

~MEDITATION~

Reading
"The Four Agreements"
by Don Miguel Ruiz

Music
"New Attitude"
by Patti LaBelle

Movie
"August: Osage County"

Week 11

Week 12

"If you are fully present in the here and the now, you need only to make a step or take a breath in order to enter the kingdom of God." –Thich Nhat Hanh

When was the last time you took a moment to watch the sun set? Got up early enough in the morning to see the sky turn from the deep blue of night to the cotton candy pink of early dawn? Can you remember the last time you stopped to watch a bird soar toward the clouds or a squirrel scamper up a tree? So, what are you waiting for? Nature awaits you!

Life Tool: For the next 7 days, at least once a day, spend some time outside. Take a walk, being sure to enjoy each step. Sit in a park and watch the wind move silently through the trees. Take off your shoes and run through dew-wet grass. Breathe deeply, making a point to honor the giver of breath.

~MEDITATION~

Reading
"Rest Is Resistance: A Manifesto"
by Tricia Hersey

Music
"Optimistic"
by Sounds of Blackness

Movie
"The Magic of Belle Isle"

Week 12

Week 13

"Disappointment results in having expectations of others that only you know about."
-La Rhonda Crosby-Johnson

What is the dream you have for your life? We often forget that our loved ones have dreams of their own. Dreams that only they've dreamed; dreams not designed by us for us. Instead of being disappointed when the lives of our spouses/lovers/partners/parents/children/siblings/friends don't meet our expectations, take a moment to find out what they dream. Our dreams only come true; really come true when we dream in color and allow others to do the same.

Life Tool: For the next 7 days, remove your expectations from those around you. Build your dream and support (whether you agree/understand/like) the dreams of others!

~MEDITATION~

Reading
"A Return To Love" and "Every Day Grace"
by Marianne Williamson

Music
"Happy Being Me"
by Anita Wilson

Movie
"The Color Purple"
(Starring Whoopi Goldberg and the musical)

Week 13

Week 14

"The journey is the destination."
-La Rhonda Crosby-Johnson

Oops. You missed it. In the frantic and chaotic lives we've created for ourselves (or allowed others to create for us), we are missing the simple, quiet moments that feed our spirits - the sound of your child splashing in the bathtub; the laughter of your best friend as you honor your relationship with a late night phone conversation or lunch at your favorite restaurant. As you hurry toward the destination, take some time to enjoy the journey. You may just discover that you've already arrived.

Life Tool: For the next 7 days, for at least 30 minutes per day, do only one thing at a time. No answering email while you listen to voice mail messages, no texting while listening to your son read his book report, no watching TV while you eat, etc.

~MEDITATION~

Reading
"Becoming" and "The Light We Carry"
by Michelle Obama

Music
"Brave"
by Sara Bareilles

Movie
"Claudine"

Week 14

Week 15
"Please take responsibility for the energy you bring into this space." –Dr. Jill Bolte Taylor

Feel like the world, or at least the people around you have all gone crazy? Do chaos, confusion, and discord stalk you like the paparazzi watching Kim Kardashian purchase maternity clothes? Keep attracting folks you'd rather not? Have you ever thought it might be the energy you bring to the situation? Looking for peace? Bring a peaceful attitude to your time with others. Want healthier relationships? Bring an open heart and positive outlook; expect the best. Are you feeling angry, anxious, fearful, guilty, sad? Set the intention that you will only bring the best of yourself into the space with others. Need to clear away some negative (or not useful) energy? First acknowledge what you're feeling is real. Your feelings can never be "right" or "wrong" they just are. Feelings are never "bad." It's what action you take because of those feelings that may not work in your favor. Take a deep breath (actually 3 really deep ones work best – inhale fully through your nose and push the air out through your mouth) and refuse to let negative energy plague you.

Life Tool: For the next 7 days be conscious of your energy. Be aware of the energy of others. Reduce the time you spend in toxic environments.

~MEDITATION~

Reading
"Anatomy of The Spirit"
by Caroline Myss

Music
"Man In The Mirror" and "Keep The Faith"
by Michael Jackson

Movie
"Hotel Rwanda"

Week 15

Week 16

"You cannot cross the sea by merely standing and staring at the water."
-Rear Admiral Michelle Howard

Don't wait another minute for life to happen to you. Make it happen for you. You don't need more money, a smaller waist line, a perfect romance. You just need to get in the water. So, go ahead, make that phone call you've been thinking about; write that book, start that new job, sign up for those classes, play hooky from work and go to a museum or see a movie, paint your toenails robin's egg blue, change your hair style, take a new route to school or work, try a new restaurant.....

Life Tool: For the next 7 days, once per day, do a new thing! Don't worry if it feels uncomfortable, most new things do.

~MEDITATION~

Reading
"The Power of Now"
by Eckhart Tolle

Music
"I Was Here" and "Break My Soul"
by Beyonce

Movie
"American Fiction"

Week 16

Week 17
"Be grateful to everyone." –Pema Chodron

Human beings do the best we can. We don't always get it "right." We make the same mistakes over and over. We hurt the ones we say we love. We ignore the truth even when it is as plain as the nose on our face. We lie. We cheat.We steal. We break promises to ourselves and others. We act when it would be better to be still and we freeze when action is the best plan. Be grateful.Be grateful for every slip along the path; for every time you fell flat on your face and had to get back up again.Be grateful for the person who betrayed you, left you, and took from you what you thought you couldn't live without.Be grateful to that person who cuts you off on the freeway, takes the last seat on the bus. Be grateful to that person who left when you wanted him/her to stay. Every situation is a lesson and every person is a teacher. Be grateful.

Life Tool: For the next 7 days remember to say "Thank You" for all things.

~MEDITATION~

Reading
"Mother To Son"
by Langston Hughs (poem)

Music
"I Didn't Know My Own Strength"
by Whitney Houston

Movie
"Shirley"
Starring Regina King

Week 17

Week 18

"The hardest battle is to be nobody but yourself in a world that is doing its best, night and day, to make you like everybody else." -e. e. cummings

Remember Junior High School (or for those of you younger than me, Middle School? That time when you ached to be an individual but never forgot to call your friends t see what they were wearing to school the next day. The weight loss and cosmetics companies are multi-Billion dollar industries. Not because their products are so wonderful or work so well, but because at one time or another we all strived to be like everybody else. You are enough. Every hair on your head (without the wig or weave) is perfect. Your lips, feet, nose, ears are the right size. If you find yourself unhappy with what you see in the mirror, do what is necessary for a healthier you. Make changes based on what is best for you and not because you're competing with the cover of the latest magazine.

Life Tool: For the next 7 days, reduce the amount of time you spend looking at magazines and commercials. Avoid comparing yourself to others. Take time to look at yourself (withou clothes and makeup) in the mirror. Run your fingers through your hair. Repeat until you ca smile and see your beauty.

~MEDITATION~

Reading
"The 40 Day Soul Fast: Your Journey to Authenticity"
by Cindy Trimm

Music
"Just Fine" and "Good Morning Gorgeous"
by Mary J. Blige

Movie
"Charlie and The Chocolate Factory"

Week 18

Week 19
"There is no flower-strewn path to success. And if there is, I have not found it, for if I have accomplished anything in life it is because I have been willing to work hard."
-Madame C. J. Walker

I know. It seems that everybody else is making it. They even make it look easy. We hear about the "overnight success" and shake our heads. We've bought the "how to be a millionaire in 30 days" books, we've taped the affirmations to our bathroom mirrors. We even buy a lottery ticket on our birthdays. Success is never "overnight." Ask someone who's successful and they'll explain just how many years of "overnights" that were involved. Success requires our full and complete participation and involvement. It takes commitment and discipline. It takes being willing to attempt and fail and attempt again. It takes patience. You will accomplish in life, only that for which you are willing to work. Success takes sacrifice. If you're not willing to do the work, stop talking about how success keeps avoiding you. If you're not working as hard as you can toward making your dream(s) a reality, then it is not success that is avoiding you, it's you that's avoiding success.

Life Tool: For the next 7 days, at least once per day, do something that moves you closer to the success you've been talking about.

~MEDITATION~

Reading
"All The Joy You Can Stand"
by Debrena Jackson Gandy

Music
"Be Grateful"
by Walter Hawkins

Movie
"The Pursuit of Happyness"

Week 19

Week 20

"Ask and it will be given to you; seek and you will find; knock and the door will be opened to you."
-Matthew 7:7

Or as the "old folks" would say, "A closed mouth don't get fed."

What are you missing, lacking in your life because you simply haven't asked?
- Does he/she love me like I love him/her?
- May I work from home 2 days a week to spend more time with my aging mother?
- How much do I need to save monthly to retire in the lifestyle that best suits me?
- How did I end up here (or back here) again?

Without asking the correct question, you'll never receive the answer you need. Maybe you're not asking the correct question because you really don't want an answer. Answers challenge us. Answers often frighten us because they make ignoring the obvious very difficult. Answers, when accepted, make change inevitable. The thought of change may send you retreating to the dark corners of your life, but guess what? You're braver, stronger, fiercer than you imagine.

Life Tool: This week ask for what you want/need.

~MEDITATION~

Reading
"Life's Spices From Seasoned Sistahs"
edited by Vicki Ward

Music
"Love Can Build A Bridge"
by The Judds

Movie
"Inside Out" and "Inside Out 2"

Week 20

Week 21

"Just do what works for you because there will always be someone who thinks differently." -Michelle Obama

We expend a lot of energy getting along with (or trying to get along with) other people. We worry about whether our or not our spouse/lovers/partners love us. Do our children respect us? What do the neighbors think about our new fence or the music they heard coming out of our bedroom window? How much time have you spent wondering what YOU think of YOU?

Life Tool: This week, during your quiet time, reflect on one of the following questions each day.

1. Who am I? (Avoid answering this question with what you do or a function of a role you have.)
2. How does what I say I believe show up/manifest in my life?
3. What thoughts and behaviors do I have that no longer tell the truth of who I am now?
4. What have I failed to forgive?
5. What was I born to do?
6. If I died today, what would people say about the way I lived my life?
7. What brings me joy? (Joy is not the same as happiness. Happiness is dependent, determined and dictated by circumstances. Joy is a permanent state of being well even in the face of adversity.)

~MEDITATION~

Reading
"Left To Tell"
by Immaculee Ilibagiza

Music
"I'm Gonna Be Ready"
by Yolanda Adams

Movie
"The Fire Inside"

Week 21

Week 22

"Say no when you want to say no, and yes when you want to say yes." -Don Miguel Ruiz

People "getting in your lane?" Are you feeling ignored, disrespected? Maybe you're feeling overwhelmed and unappreciated. One reason could be that you're not telling the truth...to yourself or anyone else. You've gotten into the habit of saying what you think others want you to say; doing what others want you to do; being what others want you be. STOP IT! Give yourself permission to take some time to figure out what YOU want to say, do, be and then SAY IT! DO IT!BE IT!

Life Tool: For the next 7 days, pause before committing to requests for your time, service, money, etc. Ask yourself if answering "YES" is truly what you want. Will your "YES" answer benefit the recipient or are you just "going along to get along?" Give yourself permission to say "NO" (lovingly of course) when the best answer is truly "NO ."

~MEDITATION~

Reading
"The Book of NO"
by Susan Newman

Music
"Home"
by Stephanie Mills

Movie
"The Last Days of Ptolemy Grey"

Week 22

Week 23

"There is no courage where you do not bring your heart." –La Rhonda Crosby-Johnson

Think you're tough? Maybe you see yourself as a "strong" woman. Do you love freely and without expectation and condition? Do you love with the intention of giving love and not with what will this action bring me? If you cannot answer "yes" to these questions then you may not be as tough/strong as you imagined. It could be that your definition of what it means to be strong and courageous could use some re-vamping. It takes courage to bring your heart to situations and circumstances that might leave it broken. There is no courage needed if there is nothing to lose. It is impossible to take a risk without your heart. So today, be courageous and take your heart into every situation and conversation. Dare to love the unlovable. Dare to show up without your armor, sword raised, ready for battle. Dare to risk any pain you anticipate for the possibility of joy.

Life Tool: For the next 7 days, go into conversations with an open heart. Be prepared to listen even when it may be difficult. Avoid battling just for the sake of battling. Re-vamp your definition of courage and strength to fit who you are today.

~MEDITATION~

Reading
"Stay In Your Lane"
by Karen Mills-Francis

Music
"Good As Hell" and "Special"
by Lizzo

Movie
"Kung Fu Panda"

Week 23

Week 24
"We are made for this moment."
-President Barack Obama

Think you can't do it, make it, figure it out, get over it, or get through it? Well, you're wrong. Every moment before this one got you ready for just this time. What did you think all those previous lessons were for?Now the test is here. This is not the time to doubt yourself or what you know.It is not the time to worry or become angry over what you don't know or have. You have everything you need to do this thing or you wouldn't be here. So, go ahead and close the door to the pity party and use your lessons to pass the test. Don't worry. You can't fail. You can only add another lesson learned.

Life Tool: For the next 7 days, take at least 10 minutes to use the matrix below to help you with a current issue in your life.

Issue	What makes this an issue for me at this time?	What experience and/or information do I have about this issue?	Who can support me?	What is the worst thing that can happen if I don't take action?	If I weren't afraid, what would I do?	What's my hope for this situation?

~MEDITATION~

Reading
"The Power to Prosper: 21 Days to Financial Freedom"
by Michelle Singletary

Music
"Little Miss"
by Sugarland

Movie
"The Woman King"

Week 24

Week 25
"If you know what hurts you, you know what hurts others." –African Proverb

Everyone has a story.Something they tell themselves everyday about who they are and who they think they are. Everyone has a past. Everyone has experienced something that has caused them great joy or as I like to say something that "would make you walk down the yellow line in the middle of the road talking to people no one can see but you." You are not the only person who has felt abandoned, betrayed, cheated, abused or misused. You are not the only person who has felt unloved or been unloving. Stop behaving like only your pain matters. Show some compassion. Share a smile or a kind word with a stranger. Find that difficult? Start with being a little kinder to yourself.

Life Tool: For the next 7 days, at least once per day, make real (face-to-face) contact with another human being. Listen without an agenda to a co-worker. Sit with a friend who just needs someone near. Share some time finding out what excites your child.Ask your bank teller or the clerk in the post office how they are. Take the time to say "good morning" to the person taking your triple mocha latte order.

~MEDITATION~

Reading
"Their Eyes Were Watching God"
by Zora Neale Hurston

Music
"Moon Meets the Sun"
by Our Native Daughters

Movie
"Winter's Tale"

Week 25

Week 26
"Dreams don't have deadlines."
-LL Cool J

It is never too late to become what you've always wanted to become. It's never too late to learn something new or attempt something you've watched others do. It's never too late to turn the dream of your life into your life. BE what you dream and don't worry about how "late" you think it is. Like the birth of a baby or the baking of a cake (before the microwave kind), dreams happen when they're ready. So, put your clock away and step into the center of your dreamed about life.

Life Tool: For the next 7 days, take some time each day to remember what you dreamed for yourself and then make a plan to set that dream in motion.

~MEDITATION~

Reading
"Whatever Happened To Daddy's Little Girl"
by Jonetta Rose Barras

Music
"Invincible"
by Kelly Clarkson

Movie
"Akeelah and the Bee"

Week 26

Week 27

"When it comes down to what really matters, we are all on the same path." -Oprah Winfrey

Over twenty years ago I created a workshop activity titled "How Different Are We?" for a group of clinic workers who really didn't like teenagers and had been recently charged with expanding reproductive health services to teenagers! My traveling teen panel, which I usually took along with me to workshops specifically addressing teen issues, was in the middle of standardized testing in their schools and couldn't get away. How would I, a non-teenager, be able to get these health professionals to really SEE teens? While we focus easily and quickly on the differences between us, we sometimes forget to recognize, acknowledge and appreciate our similarities. When we do this we miss the opportunity to connect to another human being; we waste the gift of diversity. So, the next time you find yourself separating folks into "them" and "us" take some time to look for what you have in common.

Life Tool: For the next 7 days, find opportunities to connect, understand, acknowledge and appreciate the similarities you have with someone you perceive as "different." At the end of the 7 days, take 5 minutes to journal what you discovered about yourself.

~MEDITATION~

Reading
"Set Boundaries, Find Peace: A Guide To Reclaiming Yourself"
by Nedra Glover Tawwab

Music
"I Hope You Dance"
by Lee Ann Womack or Gladys Knight

Movie
"Alice"
Starring Keke Palmer

Week 27

Week 28

"We who sometimes drown in words could afford to learn that sometimes the deepest relationships are built without them." -Edward M. Kennedy

When was the last time you spent a quiet evening at home? Sat with a friend or loved one without talking? Listened without agenda or waiting to respond? The noise of our daily lives is drowning out the important sounds we need to hear – our own inner whisperings; the urging or response of The Creator. It doesn't always take saying something to convey a feeling or thought. There is untapped power in your silence. Use it!

Life Tool: This week spend some time with a family member or friend in silence. At the end of the week take 5 minutes to journal what you "heard."

~MEDITATION~

Reading
"Women's Bodies, Women's Wisdom: Creating Physical and Emotional Health & Healing"
by Christiane Northrup

Music
"I'm Every Woman"
by Chaka Khan or Whitney Houston

Movie
"Respect"
Starring Jennifer Hudson

Week 28

Week 29
"Afraid to appear selfish, we lose our self."
-Julia Cameron

There's a huge misconception about self-care. Faulty socialization and what I sometimes th
must be some diabolical master plan to keep women from their innate power, has program
many of us to feel guilt or shame when we take time to care for ourselves. We even go so fa
to be angry with other women who have been brave and sensible enough to move outside
this teaching! Stop it right now! The words "selfish" and "self-care" don't belong in the sar
sentence together. If you struggle with the idea of taking care of yourself first, then ask you
why everyone else is more important than you? That is exactly what you are saying when
put the needs of others before yours, even when it risks your well being. Now this doesn't m
run away from home or quit your job to walk aimlessly along the beach. It just means that
deserve the best care, too....just like everybody that you care for. This may mean that you
sister who just can't seem to get it together may have to get a second job to take care of her
children while you use the money you earned and saved to go to that meditation retreat
cruise. Your teenage and adult children may have to do their own laundry or fix their ow
meals while you go to a movie with a friend or take those salsa lessons you've dreamed ab
for years. Maybe it means you hire someone to come in once a week to clean for an ailing el
so you can spend some time soaking in a bubble bath. Maybe your toddlers and school-ag
children need an earlier bedtime (please tell me they already have a bedtime!) so you can h
an hour of peace and quiet before your bedtime. Whether we want to admit it or not, if w
don't take care of ourselves well, really well, we won't be around to take care of all those fo
anyway. The flight attendants have it right, "Put on your own oxygen mask first."

Life Tool: This week make a list of your responsibilities. Include everything you do for others. Is th
something someone else could do that would free up some time for self-care? Next, make a list
ways you can begin to care better for yourself and do at least one by week's end. Repeat often!

~MEDITATION~

Reading
"Broken Open"
by Elizabeth Lesser

Music
"Touching Peace"
by Keiko Matsui

Movie
"Becoming Jane"
Starring Anne Hathaway

Week 29

Week 30

"Every day we awake with a certain amount of mental, emotional and physical energy that we spend throughout the day. If we allow our emotions to deplete our energy, we have no energy to change our lives or to give to others."
-Don Miguel Ruiz

Be honest. There are some people and situations that suck you dry. I always think of the ol vampire movies (haven't watched enough of the new ones) when the vampire sucks all th blood out of someone, leaving them in a pale and colorless heap on the floor. Ever have to "psyche" yourself out or "gear up" to be in the company of someone? That's what I'm talkir about. There are folks that energize and nurture you and then there are the others. They'r not mean people. We've loved many of them for years. They can even be fun and exciting They just run on empty so much that they rob us or our energy. Most of the time, trying to "be nice", we don't even tell them this is our experience of them. It's your (mental, emotion physical) energy. You get to decide how much of it you want to use for the good of others ar yourself and how much you want to waste on the energy vampires. There is a limited amount available, so use your energy wisely.

Life Tool: For the next 7 days, pause 3 times per day, to see where you are focusing/spending yo energy. Are you in the company of "energy vampires?" Do you need to find a way to replenish you energy supply?

Some Energy Vampires	Some Ways To Replenish Your Energy
"Needy" people	Reduce time around the folks who suck you dry.
Ignoring your feelings for the sake of "being nice."	Say YES only when you want to say YES.
Gossip	Disengage from meaningless and/or hurtful conversations. "Just listening" counts.
Holding a position for the sake of being "right."	Be willing to look at a situation from another perspective.

~MEDITATION~

Reading
"Awaken: 100 Questions To Expand Your Mind and Open Your Heart" by Joseph M. Bernard, Ph.D.

Music
"Hear My Call" and "Golden" by Jill Scott

Movie
"Harriet"

Week 30

Week 31
Adversity introduces a man to himself." –
Marcus Lattimore, Running back, University of
South Carolina

For many of us, life hasn't been a bed of roses. To put it simply, life has just been plain old hard. Growing up, I would sometimes hear my father and uncles say, "If I didn't have bad luck, I wouldn't have any luck at all." What I've come to learn, through and because some of that "bad" stuff is that life was not designed to be easy It was designed to teach you what you needed to learn to do what you came here to do. Some of us had to repeat a lesson or two along the way. Some of us felt we failed so miserably we "checked out" for a while and "hid" in places of anger, sadness and/or reckless and harmful behaviors. The only way out of those hard times is often through them. While moving through, you get an up close and personal look at yourself. It's an opportunity for you to evaluate skill and character levels. You get to "meet" yourself in a whole new way.

Life Tool: This week find an autobiography or biography of someone who has met adversity See what skills they acquired as they went through the challenges. What can you learn and/or use in your life?

~MEDITATION~

Reading
"The 5 Commandments of Self-Love"
by Tiffany A. Wright, MSW

Music
"Because You Loved Me"
by Celine Dion

Movie
"Set It Off"

Week 31

Week 32
"When Light remembered her name, the Shadows parted." –Fana from My Soul To Take

It isn't that you're not brilliant. It is merely that you've forgotten. You've lost your way. Things have been too dark for too long and you've gotten used to it. You've found some safety and comfort there in the dark. Darkness is neither who you are nor where you belong. Cast your light and watch what happens. Watch the thoughts, habits and relationships of the darkness begin to fade away. Take a look at all you can see now that you've allowed the light to shine again. Once the light is back on you may have to spruce yourself up a bit, but that's okay. You were made to be brilliant!

Life Tool: For the next 7 days refuse to play small. Accept compliments and support with "thank you." Allow yourself to admit when you've done something well. Find something at which you excel and then write yourself a note about how fantastic it is!

~MEDITATION~

Reading
"Finding Me"
by Viola Davis

Music
"Beautiful Girl"
by Sarah McLachlan

Movie
"Hugo"

Week 32

Week 33
"Live so that when your children think of fairness and integrity they think of you."
-H. Jackson Brown, Jr.

Most of us heard it when we were growing up…"Do as I say and not as I do." It didn't work then and it doesn't work now. Children learn by what they see and hear and just as easily from what they don't see or hear. If we want our children to "be better" then we're going to have to "woman up" and do the hard work of being better ourselves. Time to heal the old wounds. Time to stop inflicting pain on yourself and others. Time to look for ways to be kinder and love stronger. Time to accept an apology and ask for forgiveness. Time to be what we want our children to be.

Life Tool: For the next 7 days be conscious of your language around your children (and the children in your world.) Watch what you do in front of them. Make sure what you say is what you do.

~MEDITATION~

Reading
"Finding Your Way in a Wild New World: Reclaim Your True Nature to Create the Life You Want"
by Martha Beck

Music
"I Am Light"
by India.Arie

Movie
"Hidden Figures"

Week 33

Week 34
"You cannot change what you did not get."
–Juanita Littlejohn

"I'm so sorry." Many of us have been waiting to hear these 3 words all our lives. Whether it was a father who walked away or pretended not to be there even when he came home every night or a mother who refused to hug us for fear that we wouldn't be prepared for the "tough, cruel" world, "I'm so sorry." Maybe it was the lover/spouse/partner who promised he/she would be there forever and then changed his/her mind and left when you needed him/her the most. It could have been that beloved child(ren) you sacrificed everything for only to have them live a life that is beneath what you expected. "I'm so sorry." We can't go back and change a thing. We have only what's in front of us. Your yesterday is gone. Write your story for today!

Life Tool: For the next 7 days, don't tell that story again. You know the one. The one in which you talk about all that "they" did to you.

~MEDITATION~

Reading
"The Places that Scare you: A Guide to Fearlessness in Difficult Times"
by Pema Chodron

Music
"Try"
by Colbie Caillat

Movie
"The First Wives Club"

Week 34

Week 35

"When they were hungry, you gave them bread from heaven and water from a rock when they were thirsty." –Nehemiah 9:15

It looks impossible. There is no obvious way or way out. Now what? Expect a miracle. That's the only thing that will match this predicament. Don't look for waters to part or bushes to flame without being consumed. Miracles come in all shapes and sizes. How will you KNOW when it happens? Easy. It will be the very thing you thought was impossible occurring in front of your eyes.

Life Tool: For the next 7 days, take time to reflect on the miracles in your life and give thanks.

~MEDITATION~

Reading
"The Seven Spiritual Laws of Success: A Practical Guide to the Fulfillment of Your Dreams"
by Deepak Chopra

Music
"I Am"
by Beautiful Chorus

Movie
"Why Did I Get Married?"

Week 35

Week 36

"A fish cannot drown in water. A bird does not fall in the air. Each creature God made must live in its own true nature." -Mechthild of Magdeburg

How long has it been since you've created something? How long has it been since you took the time to stop attempting to fit into the molds made by others and dared to create your own space? Find your element. There is a unique gift, talent, understanding that only YOU bring to the planet. Don't worry about what it will look like to others. Don't give a single minute of thought to what they might whisper behind your back. Don't even worry if at first it doesn't make sense to you. Just do it and be glad!

Life Tool: Once a day for the next 7 days create something just for yourself. Maybe it will be a song you sing out loud in the shower.Maybe you'll buy spices you can't pronounce to make a recipe you saw on TV. Maybe you'll sit in the middle of the floor and draw a picture or color in your child's coloring book......

~MEDITATION~

Reading
"How To Relax"
by Thich Nhat Hanh

Music
"What's Going On?"
by Marvin Gaye

Movie
"Moana"

Week 36

Week 37

"You did then what you knew to do, and when you knew better, you did better." -Maya Angelou

This quote saved my (emotional) life. It stopped me immediately from worrying and blaming and fretting over something I wished I'd done. It allowed me to forgive myself in the present moment for past decisions. There was something so loving about this quote. It was big enough to swallow up all the petty punishments I'd put i place for myself because I thought I "should've known better." Well I didn't know better, at least until I did know better. And guess what? When I did know better I wa able to make the necessary changes and corrections. I did better. I've come to believ that everyone is doing the best they can with what they have. Why wouldn't they? Maybe you have a little more than the other folks. That still doesn't change the fact that they are doing the best they can. You probably know more "now" than you did "then" but that doesn't mean you didn't make the best choice at the time. Forgive yourself for not knowing. Forgive yourself for thinking you "should've known better Acknowledge your intention to always do the best and be willing to recognize that intention in others. And please, once you know better, do better.

Life Tool: For the next 7 days, resist the urge to blame yourself for past decisions. Forgive yourself. Ask forgiveness of those who were harmed by your lack of knowledge at the time Write a note to that "self" acknowledging that you recognize "you" did your best.

~MEDITATION~

Reading
"all about love"
by bell hooks

Music
"Black Butterfly"
by Deniece Williams

Movie
"A League of Their Own"

Week 37

Week 38

"Picture it. Sicily 1923."
-Sophia, from The Golden Girls

You will never arrive at your desired destination without a picture of what it will look like when you get there. I know you're busy and you stopped dreaming a long time ago. That may be why you've felt the joy slip out of your life. Could be why you feel so robotic or like that little hamster on the wheel, going around and around and around. Can't find anything to get excited about? Stuck in habits and patterns that keep you doing the same thing and getting the same results? Feel like you might be missing something? You are......a picture for your life.

Life Tool: This is going to take a couple of weeks. This week, collect the supplies you'll need: old magazines, a poster board, scissors, glue, stickers, markers, glitter, ribbons, pictures, favorite quotes, etc. Take a few minutes each day to cut out pictures that represent the new picture you'd like for your life. Dedicate space in your home to work on this project next week.

~MEDITATION~

Reading
"Shifts: An Anthology of Women's Growth Through Change"
edited by Michelle Duster and Trina Sotira with Jen Cullerton Johnson

Music
"I Found Love"
by Phyllis Hyman

Movie
"Roma"

Week 38

Week 39

"I'm starting with the man in the mirror. I'm asking him to change his ways. And no message could've been any clearer. If you wanna make the world a better place, take a look at yourself and make that change." -Michael Jackson

It begins with you. I know it would be easier if someone else would do it for you, after all you have to do everything, right? Well, our lessons don't come from the hands of others and aren't done for us. It's time. Don't worry about the outcome. Take the first step.

Life Tool: For the next 7 days, take 10 – 15 minutes each day (more if you have it) to use the materials you gathered last week to build a collage of your "dreamed about" life. Be in each moment, as you cut out the pictures, glue them to the poster board, and add your favorite quote or a fun sticker. Turn off the television. Put the kids to bed early. Let the calls (on all the phones!) go to voice mail. Play some soft music, burn a scented candle. Display the new picture of your life in a place where you can see it daily!

~MEDITATION~

Reading
"Phenomenal Woman"
by Maya Angelou (poem)

Music
"You're Next In Line For A Miracle"
by Shirley Caesar

Movie
"Waiting To Exhale"

Week 39

Week 40
"Celebrate. Play. Aim High. Dream. Teach."
-A few words from my Dream Board

What are you busy doing? What do you think about the life you're living? Is it filled with obligations and chores? Are you wasting time to avoid what must be done? Are you filled with joy just at the thought of a new day? With each day we get another chance. Yesterday is done. Life is happening right now, so if you've been waiting for to happen....This Is It. Celebrate those small moments that you usually take for granted. Make some time to play. I know you're busy but remember this is truly the only time you have. Aim High. Stop accepting second place or taking the first thing that comes along just because it showed up. Dream. It is only possible if you first imagine. Teach. Your lessons were not meant just for you. Time to show someone els the way.

Life Tool: For the next 7 days take 10 minutes each day to set some goals for the next 3 months. Be sure to set goals in each area of your life for holistic wellbeing: 1) Financial, 2) Physical, 3) Friendships and Family 4) Work, 5) Community and 6) Spiritual. Share your goals with someone you trust and who will support you in attaining these goals.

~MEDITATION~

Reading
"The Alchemist"
by Paulo Coelho

Music
"No More Rain"
by Angie Stone

Movie
"The Joy Luck Club"

Week 40

Week 41

"Blood don't make you family."
-La Rhonda Crosby-Johnson, Khadija Washington

Whoever said, "You can't choose your family" was so wrong. I came to know family in the broadest sense of the word at a very early age. Many of my aunts, uncles, cousins, nieces, nephews, sisters, brothers, daughters and sons were not connected to me by bloodlines. Family has absolutely nothing to do with biology. Sometimes our family tree is filled with people who cannot or will not love us in the way that we need. Sometimes our family tree is filled with people who misunderstand and betray us and each other. Rather than spending time trying to get them to be what we want and need accept the fact that maybe your sisters and brothers were born t other parents. Stop playing victim to feelings that your family should be there for you because you have parents in common or share strands of DNA. Who are the people in your life that have nurtured you; had your best interest at heart no matte what? Who do you call first to share your greatest triumphs and tragedies? Who would you crawl out of your warm bed in the middle of the night to sit with just because they can't sleep? That's family.

Life Tool: For the next 7 days do some forgiveness work. Write a letter to the family member(s) that haven't been the family you needed. Forgive them for being unable to meet your needs. Once this is done, shred it. It's not meant for them – this is your work. Now take inventory of the people placed in your life through love and circumstance. Creat your own family tree.

~MEDITATION~

Reading
"Between The Dark and The Daylight"
by Sister Joan Chittister

Music
"Beautiful U R"
by Deborah Cox

Movie
"Whale Rider"

Week 41

Week 42

"We are not the same persons this year as last nor are those we love. It is a happy chance if we changing continue to love the changed person."
-W. Somerset Maugham

Things change. People change. Sometimes what we thought might last forever end before "forever." There is no way around the pain that comes when "it just doesn' work." There is a way through the pain and that is to accept and acknowledge the en It doesn't mean the other person is "bad" or that we even have to be angry or ever that something has to go terribly "wrong." We just have to know when and how to walk away with grace, so that we don't cause unnecessary pain; so that we don't tak away from the wonder and beauty of the beginning. We don't always come togethe and stay together. We grow at different rates and in different ways. It doesn't mean that everything that came before the end wasn't real. Let's learn how to part with dignity and allow the other person to do the same.

Life Tool: For the next 7 days, evaluate your "endings." Ask yourself the following questions to guide your reflection:

- Did I hold on too long?
- Did I miss an earlier sign that it was over?
- Did I set up a situation to get them to end it because I couldn't?
- How did I feel once it was over?
- What are the similarities in my "beginnings" and "endings?"
- What did I learn about myself that I can take to the next relationship?

~MEDITATION~

Reading
"The Woman Code"
by Sophia Nelson

Music
"I Rise"
by Etana

Movie
"Thelma and Louise"

Week 42

"Your crown has been bought and paid for. All you have to do is put it on your head." –James Baldwin

The battle has been won. You are here. Some of us have been struggling, fighting, trying for so long that we didn't notice when we won. There is a whole new way to walk when you know the battle is finished. Put away your weapons. Take off all that armor. Stop looking for "the enemy" around every corner. Get your head in that crown. It's yours!

Life Tool: For the next 7 days, at least once per day, look for "the wins" and stop fighting.

~MEDITATION~

Reading
"Care of The Soul"
by Thomas Moore

Music
"Ain't No Stoppin' Us Now"
by McFadden & Whitehead

Movie
"Black Panther"

Week 43

Week 44

"Real knowledge is to know the extent of one's ignorance." -Confucius

It is okay not to know. It is amazing what you will learn if you don't already think (or behave) as if you know it all. Take a moment and listen to the idea or opinion of someone else. Ask someone what they think about something. Breathe through the fear that will most certainly come up when you accept that you don't have the answers to everything, all the time.   Quiet the loudmouth critic in your mind that may come to tell you how "stupid" you are for not knowing. Set aside the pride you allow yourself to feel when you know something someone else doesn't. The most powerful answer you will ever give in your life is "I don't know." Try it and see where it takes you.

Life Tool: For the next 7 days approach even familiar situations with a new and curious eye. Look for what you may have missed before. Challenge yourself to see things in a new way.

~MEDITATION~

Reading
"Until Today"
by Iyanla Vanzant

Music
"Rise Up"
by Andra Day

Movie
"Erin Brockovich"

Week 44

Week 45
"If you hate a person, you hate something in him/her that is a part of yourself. What isn't part of ourselves doesn't disturb us." –Herman Hesse

Ouch! Our perfection is a fantasy that keeps us from healing. We dress up real well and to others we look like we've got it all together. We smile when we would rather curse someone out. We tell a lie to avoid confrontation. We stay when leaving is the only thing that really makes sense. We leave when we believe we could have tried a little harder. We eat/drink/have meaningless sex instead of acknowledging how tired/sad/angry/afraid/ashamed/guilty we are. We have pretended that everything is all right for so long that we've come to believe the lie. We have been so successful at masking our brokenness that we cannot count how many times we've excused it by saying, "That's just the way I am." What hurts is so deeply hidden that we don't recognize that the very thing that "works our last remaining nerve" or "ticks us off" in that other woman is the thing we've buried in ourselves.

Life Tool: For the next 7 days, notice those folks that "get on your nerves." Ask yourself the following questions: What is it about ME that make this person difficult for me? What might I learn about myself if I stop "hating" her/him?

~MEDITATION~

Reading
"The Art of Stillness"
by Pico Iyer

Music
"Someday We'll All Be Free"
by Donny Hathaway

Movie
"The Queen of Katwe"

Week 45

Week 46
"But no woman can love a weak man hard enough to make him strong." Blue Hamilton from "Just Wanna Testify" –by Pearl Cleage

I have yet to meet a woman who has not tried this before; at least once. As we say, "Been there. Done That." After all, we're capable, able and strong. We've been raised to take care of ourselves; do what must be done; hold it together. In all our trying to make him better; make him responsible; make him accountable what has happened to too many of us is that we've left pieces of ourselves along the way. It isn't our fault that he won't get or can't keep a job, had a baby with the woman whose kids you babysit, started using drugs and/or alcohol, won't commit to his children, etc. As capable, able and strong as we are we cannot do for someone what they are unable or unwilling to do for themselves. Now this does not mean that we should run out of the brother that is giving it his all and having some bad luck. I'm talking about compromising what you know is right, to try and make him better. I'm talking about denying the truth that is before you, just so he'll stay. I'm talking about ignoring your feelings just so he won't become angry. It's time to gather up the pieces of yourself. Make some decisions that are good for you. Get some help if the situation is dangerous or could become dangerous. It's time to be strong – not for him. For you!

Life Tool: For the next 7 days, evaluate the current state of your relationship. Be honest enough with yourself and your spouse/partner/lover to see what's working and what might not be working. Not currently in a relationship and thrilled? Share what you are learning with another woman. Not currently in a relationship and you want to be in one? Review your last 3 and gather up your pieces!

~MEDITATION~

Reading
"Emotional Freedom"
by Judith Orloff

Music
"Stand"
by Goapele

Movie
"Daughters of The Dust"

Week 46

Week 47
"Stay in your lane."
-Judge Karen Mills-Francis

This simple phrase has become a mainstay in our lexicon over the last several years. We say it [without even thinking. I use it as a reminder to do what my daddy told me to do when I was a y[oung] girl; "mind my own business." We know it works when driving at or over the speed limit on t[he] highway, but how do we put this into practice in our daily lives? How do we know when we're o[ut of] our lane? Here are a few examples:

How We Know We're Out of Our Lane	How To Stay In Your Lane
We spend more time thinking and talking about other people's lives.	Focus the majority of your energy on your life and give up thinking you can control everything.
We give advice and opinion when not asked	Listen without offering an opinion.
We are angry, upset, hurt about the actions or decisions of someone else.	Reduce your emotional investment in what others choose to do for themselves.
We are overwhelmed, fatigued, burned out physically, emotionally, financially because of others.	Practice self-care. Put yourself back into the center of your own life and learn to say "No."

I can hear all your reasons for not staying in your lane. Stop yourself. The world will not stop spi[nning] if your 7 year old daughter gets caught without her raincoat; your homebound mother or father [has to] eat the same thing two days in a row because you decide to stay home and garden; your teen or y[oung] adult child's cell phone is cut off because they chose to use the money for the phone bill to go t[o a] social event with friends. There is peace and quiet in your lane. Put on your signal and get ov[er].

Life Tool: For the next 7 days, LET GO. Take some time each day to separate the stuff in your lane from [the] stuff in everyone else's lane. What are you doing that someone can do for him/herself? What problems [are] you solving that really aren't yours to solve? Breathe well because just the thought of letting go can ca[use] some of us to hyperventilate.

~MEDITATION~

Reading
"More Myself"
by Alicia Keys

Music
"I Am"
by Kindred the Family Soul

Movie
"Happy Feet"

Week 47

Week 48

Life is really simple. We insist on making it complicated." -Confucius

Let's clean up a bit. It's time to remove some things from your space/life and make ro for something new. What do you really need? What are you putting in front of the thing(s) you really need to do? What are you adding to "the mix" that is weighing yo down? What keeps you from soaring above the melee? What are you avoiding, denyi overlooking, ignoring? What are you focusing way too much energy on? What are yo forcing? What are you telling yourself about why things aren't going your way? Wh are you doing about it?

Life Tool: For the next 7 days, dedicate at least 15 minutes each day to clearing some spac
- Go through that drawer you haven't opened in years and toss out what you don't nee
- Inventory your closet(s). What aren't you using; wearing that would bless someone else? Hint: if you haven't worn it in the last 12 months chances are you won't.
- Open mail and discard the junk.
- Go through old business cards, files, phone books and get rid of the things you don't need/use anymore.
- Put some order to those kitchen cupboards.
- Clean off that desk or the foot of your bed.
- Have a garage sale with all the stuff you thought you needed in your storage unit.
- Donate some appliances and electronics to a local school or shelter.
- Tell someone goodbye and farewell.

~MEDITATION~

Reading
"I Know Why The Caged Bird Sings"
Maya Angelou

Music
"Control"
by Janet Jackson

Movie
"Frozen"

Week 48

Week 49
"Tomorrow there will be sun."
-Gabourey Sidibe

It is not as bad as it seems. Or maybe it is. However, the world did not stop rotating on its axis. The sun did not fall from the sky. The moon and the stars did not stop shining. The only thing to do when it seems bad or really, truly is bad is to hold on.

Life Tool: For the next 7 days avoid catastrophic thinking (unless there is a real catastrophe and then accept the truth!)BREATHE through it and hold on.....this too shall pass. (Hint: A long line at Starbucks, missing your manicure/pedicure appointment, your child flunking a spelling test, someone cutting you off on the freeway, a disagreement with family/friend is NOT a catastrophe.)

~MEDITATION~

Reading
"A Year To Live: How to Live This Year as If it Were Your Last"
by Stephen Levine

Music
"Somewhere Over The Rainbow"
by Joey Alexander

Movie
"Frida"

Week 49

Week 50

"Focusing your life solely on making a buck shows a certain poverty of ambition.
asks too little of yourself. Because it's only when you hitch your wagon to somethi
larger than yourself that you realize your true potential." –President Barack Oba

Of course the rent has to be paid, Little Joey needs new shoes, the lights are best when they com
when you flip the switch and your car does not run on love. But life is so much more than the m
There is no arguing the fact that having money provides us with additional options, opportunitie
comforts. Dodging the repo man and staying up late wondering how you'll pay your child's sch
tuition is stressful. So many of us live on the edge of financial ruin or have for so long that we t
the numbers to the Powerball lottery will make all our ills dissolve. We were meant to do more
just make money. We were meant to add our very unique gifts and talents to this thing called lif
were meant to do only what we can do to make this place better, not just for ourselves and our fa
and friends, but for those who will come centuries after we're gone. So, today don't sell yours
cheap.

Life Tool #1: For the next 7 days take a good look at your financial situation. What you actually do over
next week will depend on where you are in your financial development. Here are some ideas if you're no
where to begin.

- Review your current budget (if you don't have one, time to create one!!)
- Balance your checkbook (or reconcile your online banking statements)
- Distinguish your "wants" from your "needs."
- Develop a systematic way to save each month and set monthly, quarterly and annual savings goals.
- Get credit card debt under control (if you don't have any give yourself a pat on the back!)
- Seek professional help. Meet with retirement professionals.
- Have a conversation with your spouse/partner about your financial realities.
- Put yourself on a buying diet for 30 days. (Only purchase what you absolutely need to live that month and take your crec
  cards out of your purse.)
- Keep a spending journal for 30 days.
- Roll all loose change and deposit into a savings account.
- Have a conversation with children about finances. Get them involved. Maybe they can save for that new video game or c
- Reflect on what you tell yourself about why you don't save and/or have the money you need to live. Look for excuses an
  rid of them.

Life Tool #2 – Once during the next 7 days spend at least one hour volunteering or doing something f
someone for which there is no monetary reward or expected return.

~MEDITATION~

Reading
"The Autobiography of Angela Davis"

Music
"Believing In Me" by Monica

Movie
"Mulan"

Week 50

Week 51
"Half of what's wrong with people today is that they ain't got no place to go that makes them peaceful. -"Willie from The Twelve Tribes of Hattie.

I was a loud, talkative child. I remember my mother uttering the words, "Please be quiet. I can't hear myself think" more times than I can count. At the time I wasn't sure why what she was thinking was more important than what I had to say to her, but as I grew older, it became crystal clear. At least Mama knew by 9pm I'd be in bed and that whether or not she was finished watching television or not, it would go off. (If you don't remember television going off, ask a parent or grandparent.)There would be peace in the house that she could look forward to each day. Can you say the same? What thoughts aren't you hearing? Do you know or remember what "peaceful" feels like? Do you know the things/activities/people that bring you a sense of peace? What have you allowed to steal, invade your peaceful place?Peace isn't always the absence of turbulence. I've come to understand it more as a place within myself that remains calm and steady even in the midst of crazy. If you have yet to discover or maybe you've just forgotten what brings you peace, take some time this week to discover or reunite yourself with your peaceful place.

Life Tool: For the next 7 days spend at least 15 minutes in complete silence. Turn off cell phones, televisions, radios, etc.See what you hear in the quiet. (Hint: If you have a commute, turn the radio off!) Create a daily ritual that invites peacefulness.

~MEDITATION~

Reading
"Zen Mind, Beginner's Mind"
by Shunryh Suzuki

Music
"Bag Lady"
by Erykah Badu

Movie
"The No. 1 Ladies' Detective Agency"

Week 51

Week 52

"Your journey does not begin on your neighbor's path."
–La Rhonda Crosby-Johnson

There are no two people just alike. There is even some evidence that identical twins have some distinct characteristics. So why do you expect the life of someone else? Why are you attempting to answer your questions with the answers that belong to others? Role models and mentors are great to have. They can provide guidance and create environments that support our growth, but they can't do it for us. You may learn which road to take by watching the journey of others. You may even avoid some unnecessary pitfalls, but you have a path that is all yours; a path that has been uniquely designed just for you. While your path may resemble the path of many others, it is not their path. They can only provide you with so much information because they don't have the information or experience needed for your path. There are experiences and lessons along your path that are created just for you. So, go ahead. Take that first step. If you fear you'll grow weary, don't. There will be a resting place just up the road. Feeling lonely? Friends will appear just when you need them most. Took a wrong turn? Guides are just waiting for you to ask for direction. Each step you take is your own. So, get moving. The journey begins.....

Life Tool: For the next 7 days, be your own counsel. Make your own decisions. Choose based on what you know to be true, right, good, etc.

~MEDITATION~

Reading
"The Hill We Climb"
by Amanda Gorman (poem)

Music
"Celebrate"
by Jordin Sparks

Movie
"American Violet"

Week 52